Special Needs, Special

Matheu James Harris Sr.

ISBN 979-8-88943-274-6 (paperback)
ISBN 979-8-88943-276-0 (hardcover)
ISBN 979-8-88943-275-3 (digital)

Christian Faith Publishing
832 Park Avenue
Meadville, PA 16335
www.christianfaithpublishing.com

Printed in the United States of America

*To my daughter, Reigna Harris, aka my special princess,
diagnosed with DiGeorge syndrome at birth.
You will always be perfect to me.
God does not make mistakes.*

Wake up in the morning; there's no time to stress.
Be ready, be willing, and let God do the rest.

Princess! Get up, it's time to get dressed.
What clothes are we choosing?
She gets dressed to impress!

We'll make your favorite breakfast,
and sit down to eat.

Wipe away the mess, then clean the sink.

JANUARY
3 4 5 6
11 12 13
18 19 20
25 26 27
Let's decorate the learning room, Princess! Up on your feet!
Let's concentrate.
Let's focus.
It's about time to think.

Good morning
Reigna.

How are you
today?

Time to get the Play–Doh.
Warm up your hands, then squish and
roll it between your fingers.
Now do a little dance.

11

Let's talk about the lesson.
Let's go get you a snack.

14

It is still bright outside when she wakes up.
The sun is setting wide.
Get your favorite shoes out, Princess.
Let's go outside!

The sun is going down!
We've been blowing bubbles for hours.
18

Bath Bombs and shower paint!
It's time for your shower.

   Daddy prepares Princess her favorite dinner: macaroni and cheese with mixed vegetables on the side.
   Time to relax and clear our heads.

We clean up one more time.
23

Get ready for bed.
24

We say our favorite bedtime prayers.
Princess asks, "Why do we do so much
special stuff every day, Daddy?"
Daddy tells little Princess...

"Because special, needs special!"
"Good night, my beautiful, special Princess."

About the Author

Matheu James Harris Sr. was born in Northern California. He attended public schools and loved math. His passion for writing developed later in life. He grew up playing soccer and loved fishing. During his high school years, he was in band and played the saxophone. He also played football and ran track. He developed a love for the muscle structure of the human body and studied physical therapy with an emphasis on sports injuries.

He is married and a father of four children. In his spare time, he loves fishing with his son and taking the family on camping trips. His oldest child learns differently. He learned how to maximize her learning abilities by thinking out of the box when teaching her new skills. He enjoys working with her and watching her learn. He loves the trust and innocence that the children who learn differently can display. He is a very involved father and believes parents of children who learn differently are an important part of their children's growth and learning process. He wants to encourage parents to advocate for their children since they know them best. He believes the educational team is important but that the final say remains with the parents.

He hopes to get a family dog in the future as the children get older and more responsible.